INTERNAL STRATEGIES

AKRON SERIES IN POETRY

INTERNAL STRATEGIES

Anita Feng

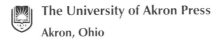 The University of Akron Press
Akron, Ohio

Acknowledgments:
5 AM: "An Offering"; *Black Warrior Review*: "To Dance Like This" (formerly titled "Like This"); *Five Fingers Review*: "China Figure"; *The Illinois Review*: "The Last Piece," "Graffiti at the Peak of Folded Brocade Hill," "An Old Recipe"; *The Madison Review*: excerpt from "Two Performances at Beihai Park"; *Nimrod*: "We Never Sleep," "China Is the Pulse of the Lungs," "Night Vision," "By the Jade Steps," "Verging," "How Still It Is Today," "China Speaks for the Moon"; *Northwest Review*: "Concerning Children," "A Letter to Beijing," "Something about Not Being Safe"; *One Meadway*: "To Lend Another Life to the Ringing of This One," "For Water Birds That Set Out without a Sea," "To Go"; *The Passionfruit Review*: excerpt from "View from the Chinese Restaurant"; *Prairie Schooner*: excerpt from "View from the Chinese Restaurant," "The Son of Heaven," "The Day Tiananmen Square Filled with Shoes," "Adolescents Assigned to Stalk Fire in Manchuria," "Growing Up on the Sly"; *Spoon River Quarterly*: "How Capable," "The Waltz Itself," "Seed," "Spring Cosmology," "Momentum," "Softness," "Will You Stay?" "Prosperous with Birds," "What Stays, What Goes"; *Xanadu*: "Cat Show in Factory #2."

"Ghost Marriage" by Anita Feng originally appeared in *Ploughshares*, Vol. 16/No. 1 (June, 1990).

"The Contortionist," an excerpt from "Two Performances at Beihai Park," first appeared in *Sojourner: The Women's Forum*, Vol. 18/No. 6 (February, 1993).

Special thanks to Michael Harper, Susan Mates, Lee Teverow, Keith Waldrop, and C. D. Wright. Also to Elton Glaser for his excellent and supportive editing.

The writing of this book has been partially funded by grants from the National Endowment for the Arts and the Illinois Arts Council, a state agency.

All inquiries and permissions requests should be addressed to the Publisher, The University of Akron Press, 374B Bierce Library, Akron, Ohio 44325-1703.

Library Of Congress Cataloging In Publication Data
Feng, Anita, 1952–
    Internal strategies / Anita Feng. — 1st ed.
      p.   cm. — (Akron series in poetry)
      ISBN 1-884836-13-5 (alk. paper). — ISBN 1-884836-14-3 (pbk.: alk. paper)
    I. Title.   II. Series.
    PS3556.E474I58   1995
    811'.54 — dc20   95-24378
                                                                      CIP

First Edition

for my husband, Nick (Xiao Ge)

CONTENTS

PROLOGUE

China Speaks for the Moon

Truly, the sun and moon wish to be light,
but the floating clouds cover them.
—Huai-nan-tzu, Book Eleven

As a child, she lights a candle in the closet
and sets out an arrangement
of porcelain fish. She wants to be a fly,

entering along the filaments in the wings, taking air
for a board to lie upon.

As a child, she rises with expectation, her mouth
full of vowels and sweets;
she sighs for them as she has them.

She wants to have wings, so she spills
her milk on the floor of the closet and rises to me
crying in milk.

As a child, she retreats into a cove, pushing a small boat
with her toe. All the world is what she is far from,
the fish nets hauling nothing but fish.

Perhaps she is full, and has eaten the fish herself,
imagining the easy life of a white crane in the sky.

We Never Sleep

Where the village circles,
a harbor is formed. Minnows fret and return
as the neighbor's junk divides them.

We remember the tallest buildings, our street,
our intractable way of doing things.

We have nothing to fear in longing for fish
and rice in our bowls.

At nightfall we sit outdoors
to look for one another, to sit out the night,
or to be invited in.

China Figure

My name is silk,
but in bare feet, I am napkin
for a daughter nearby.

My name is middle kingdom
yet I wait by the kitchen door
for a son to be born, light and easy, like fire
climbing the chimney flue.

Part of me is worn away
and my wig slips back.
I am bound in rush sandals worn to bare feet,
two pieces of wood. One eye erased
from waiting.

Somnambulant in daylight and alert at night,
I walk through fields.
Thickness waits on air.
My name, my pregnancy, is a cloud
burdened by imagination. The good idea of love

followed by centuries
of measuring rice, adding water, mixing blood,
draining water from the greens.

The children pass me back and forth,
a hot ember in my mouth.

I encourage them
to fold their hands on their laps,
and hold me from the flames.

Ghost Marriage

Paper stars and moon, three-tiered houses and their utensils,

fast-heated column of paper money lifted by ghosts,
the impatient and delighted spark.

Here are two houses crackling to heaven.
Tinseled, the paper rabbit lantern
springs into celebration

and from the mud bath, the ghosts
lay paper rice into their mouths,

fire dribbling down their chins with happiness. Black liquor,

double-tongued
flame and aspirations; lovely ash, a young bride,
lovely ash, a husband; their children deities, mere dreams,

play about the burial site as the last guests depart.

The Son of Heaven

A long night stayed the dawn of China's crimson day
Hundred-year hobgoblins galloped up and down.
But the people . . . oh the fragmented five hundred million
Suddenly a crowing cock illuminates the world.
—Mao Zedong

Beneath trees, ghosts sleep long
in the arms of roots
by a scattered hearth of stones.

A new China is sworn
into the scent of dirt with them.

A thin light quivers where the ant turns
through a pocket of air,
where a peasant, choked by frost
and a brittle crust of bread, can rise up
through the middle of a dream.

With two open wings, green
with inspiration, he reaches out
to sing the world. From everywhere,
and here in the airless fallen leaves
and after, he turns, reciting dawn.

I XIAO GE GAINS THE BEAUTY OF HIS LIFE AT ITS RIM

Singing at Dawn, 1953

At dawn I will
Present a document to the emperor.
I ask several times
How far the night is spent.
—Du Fu

Humidity sounds through the trees,
saturates the ground, and turns mud into a sea.

Here she twists and heaves
in the sly pull of undercurrent and distorted waves.
She labors in a torrent far into the night

as beginnings override one another, the high tide and bleeding,
the pain that she has fought and won.

She is young.
He is a colorless folded thing,
his arms burst open and dried by the air at dawn.

As she surfaces, she holds onto the boy.
On a raft, his fingers and toes. And as he cries,

she feels for his name, the poetic phrase
to plant among crowded forms,
and writes *Xiao Ge,* which means "singing at dawn."

About Brilliance

Birth leaves a residue
that slows its own pace through a dream.

Layered and embossed and brilliant,
they came as they were, flying
at the very least. *Let a hundred flowers bloom,*
let a hundred schools of thought contend!

Like poems of transformation, they believed
in the words that led them here.
But before they could memorize them all,

they had overflown the mark.
The Great Leap Forward left the food
and drink behind, with work
sweated out over growth
so close to the ground.

Like poems of endurance, they sweep
the floors at first light
and at nightfall they sweep again. Misgivings
rise like dust.

They have been feeding Xiao Ge
whatever they can find. And like a miracle,
he makes happy noises when they scrape the bowl,
when they can only come as they are.

Xiao Ge Wants to Be a Hero

I want to be like Dong Chun Rei holding his pack of dynamite
but I was born too late!
The Long March is over, and the Guomindang
and the Japanese . . .

I've lost my chance.

My composition is displayed on the school yard wall,
. . . and before he died he thought back
on his bitter life, oppressed
by brutal landlords and famine and cold . . .
But it is already too late;
everything has already occurred. I wait,

sitting on my heels at the bottom of the bridge.
I want an old man
to struggle over with a crate,
so that I might leap to his aid, but no one
needs anything today.

Last week our 3rd grade gang
stole into school to hammer each broken leg
to its table and chair, to repair and oil
every hinge to its door—

the sound inflated the darkness

like a brave advance
on enemy lines! Later, we carried off the glory
without a word to anyone, rejoicing
among ourselves for days. I hope

I will do something worthy someday,
like offer my life,
but I've probably come too late.

The Theme

What is it about illness
that arrives quietly with swollen eyelids,
then causes a child to be eclipsed
by the moon passing through his blood, the wind
knocked out of him overnight?
At least a year,
is now the confined preface
for going out to play. If strategy
is the theme, if a child has to begin
with, *if I survive . . .* , then he grows
inordinately. He gains the beauty
of his life at its rim,

and changes
as he begins to read. Insight infects
the slow and reckless orbit of days. Words
turn to him, transcribing a thin line,
whispering his defense:
you have heard
of using wings to fly;
you have not yet heard of flying
by being wingless . . .

His pranks
grow more gentle. He makes plans
for a sullen body
based on heroic Russian novels.
He reads
about an army pilot who loses a leg
but learns to walk by dancing on wood
strapped above the knee.
He reads, absorbed, and his weak limbs
are strung together with the cast
of every word.

Skating with the Boys at Beihai Park

Look at that! A flock of birds in overcoats and mittens.
They suck in the wind

and drink the blue frost. Their arms
are clouds hanging from the sky.
I have to try this. Before we leave

I have to know who gave them the push
that sends them skating a mile
before taking another breath.

Heaven turns in circles around the lake
while the earth sits firm.
Somebody, lend me skates!

If I have to cram my feet, fold my toes under
and squeeze to make them fit, I will.

They ride the vapor of the clouds,
the boys in their fathers' crisp hats
and Red Army jackets creased

to an edge of steel. They glide in formation,
staring down the rest of us! The floodlights
gleam over their shoulders

while others stay home to quibble
over dreams. I scramble over the ice.
I yoke flying dragons to my chariot

and roam beyond the four seas,
pushing a chair
with one hand behind my back.

The Day Tiananmen Square Filled with Shoes

Ah, the crowds. When Chairman Mao
waved to us from the south end of the square
                long live Chairman Mao!
my belly whirled, the sensation starved
like kissing a picture of a girl.

I was thirteen, and curious to see what it meant
to be among a million people screaming
                down with the cow's demon and snake spirit!
We rushed forward, waving our arms. I lost
my footing, even my shoes. Airborne,

the running soles of my feet
made no sound! I was carried all the way back
                nothing without ripples!
                no standard of rest!
to the Northeast, the Gate of Heavenly Peace,
struggling, before I touched the ground.

The Lost Generation

Floating on the wind,
What do I resemble?
A solitary gull
Between the heavens and the earth.
—Du Fu

I have been sent to Manchuria in a cotton jacket
patched with tape.

My father has been assigned to a cow shed
in the south; my mother,
to an outpost of the city. But the fish are at home.

The fish swim and egrets
flock to another part of the country
where the tide rips. And in a matter of time

when the heavens
think of earth, surely
they will think of me, riding
in the back of an open truck,
forty below zero.

We carry explosives
to break the trance hung over a landscape
since eternity. We carry back
the tail of the mountain on our shoulders.

Daily we drive on a frozen river
that is so clear
we can see rocks at the bottom, and birds
falling out of the blue sky
all at once. On the horizon

I see nothing
for hundreds of miles. Far off,

a train heads south, shrinking to Beijing.
How do I know

that those of us afraid of dying
are not exiles since birth
who have forgotten the way home?

Adolescents Assigned to Stalk Fire in Manchuria

After three days and nights of digging,
a hundred of us were not able to put it out.
Flame puffed out its chest
thousands of miles across

and our eyelids turned to butterflies
carved in stone.
We were of insignificant weight, the color
of charred wood.

Leaning together with spades in hand,
three girls slept fitfully as ash,
at a subtle distance
from the heat.

And when the wind changed,
their mouths
burst into flame. They shrank
to the size of small children who dream

of rising, a dream that suffocates fire
at the blink of an eye,
that confuses
everything of life with rest.

What We Know about Waves

We are beaten into a drought-hovering sky
by pans and metal spoons.

Feathers rappel down as we sparrows fly;
and peasants with carved bellies grow slogans
from the fields:

Oh, the waves of the Yangtse, one wave floats upon another.
The tide in my heart swells like the waves of the Yangtse!

We have the appetite of thieves—small wings,
thin feet for scuffing soil between furrows
closing on a seed, our beaks
the perfect fit to break it.

But we are airborne, pollinating dust, comrades
to the team the Red Guards gather up
as they irrigate old words with gongs:

Oh, the waves of the Yangtse, one wave thrusts forward another.
The tide in my heart swells like the waves of the Yangtse!

What did they ever know about waves?
Singing forever is tiresome.

There is difficulty in flying, even
for birds, and as we drop,
that difficulty flies out of our mouths and floats
in the rippling heat:

Oh, the waves of the Yangtse, one wave follows another.
The tide in my heart rips like the waves of the Yangtse!

Young man tied to a tree, we are also tied.
We are made over into paper replicas
of birds. Our eyes, our heat and thirst fan out
from the strings of old men with wooden spools.

And young people like you, thrilled
from vicarious flight, call to us:

Oh, the waves of the Yangtse, one wave hopes for another.
The tide in my heart swells like the waves of the Yangtse!

How Still It Is Today

I rest where the fields begin.

From a hesitant, dark sleeve, snow
descends with several arms and shields

on a landscape
both mistaken and brash.

I have no ideas left, no questions.

Words branch out from clouds:
I sing the ones that land
on my tongue. Like snow,

I rest where the fields begin.

Cat Show in Factory #2

We work a tedious job,
sorghum to chew and sawdust to swallow.

A comrade on the lathe was startled by a cat.
He said to it, "Have you been following
our great leader's words on guerrilla warfare?"
He held out a crust of bread, and I
grabbed it by the neck.

"Why not have something to eat?" I said.
"If you skin the cat, I'll cook it on the forge—
soy sauce, wine, a bit of sugar."

We stuffed the cat with sawdust
and propped it, well-fed, in a tree.

A girl came by, the one with a plain face
who quotes Mao in love letters
to me: "Ah kitty, what are you doing up there?"
The cat's eyes fixed on her with pins.

Growing Up on the Sly

After work the boys go out to walk
by the girls' rooms. This is how they flaunt
their equalized bodies of Mao suits:

some are pressed clean, some modified with white
exposed by a flagrant inch underneath.
For a flair in the vicinity of love,
the boys shine their bicycles `
with rags. And the girls
let them catch sight of pink, a rumor
flowing under their collars.

In the evenings they meet, then divide.
The boys blow smoke rings
and guzzle water with style.
They swarm into factions
to shout restless, heady versions of Marx.

Let them call me antirevolutionary
if I wear rumpled clothes
and study black-market textbooks at night.
I have so far to go—from geometry to calculus,
from the corner of my room to knowledge.
There is no end in sight.

Xiao Ge Speaks For China

1

She is the resident committee chairwoman
holding a broom
and we are swept into a courtyard
where she can ferret out every sigh. We struggle

to keep alert—
her evening threats as rhythmic and dull
as nursery rhymes. For hours
we run the risk of implicating ourselves
by yawning into our hands.

2

She is the gracious diplomat who opens the door
and displays an arrangement of glossy fish
layered in market stalls.
Certain ones of us
are let out into the streets.
As a gesture,

she opens her universities halfway
like cautious, ambivalent gifts
that never quite leave her hands
since it would spoil
the good effect.

3

She is a lonely old hag, watching
while I make other plans. She repairs
her words with a straight-stitch needle and thread
while I practice the running script of foreign devils.
Like sweets,

the meaningless sounds
fill my mouth, so full of vowels and aspirations
that are impossible to pronounce.

4
She intervenes as best she can.
She puts her nose in the door
and pathetic gray hairs in my tea. She directs me
through a multitude of streets where I line up
before a leaden cast of bureaucrats

and a magic show of forms.
Until I manage to slip out behind her back
and fill my lungs with air.

China Is the Pulse of the Lungs

Xiao Ge, I prepare blessings for you.
Having threaded the needle, I let the edge score
the palm of my hand.

Having mended the nib on my tongue,
I let deliberate songs fill out
until they are alike as old clothes.
Let America
teach you what it likes

but I, China, practice these blessings
before you leave me.
With so much history between words,
with the refined hindrance of bribes,
even you are struck
by the beauty of their markings—

their long tradition, the slow transformation
of empty forms, a trade wind
breathing through the window as your mother sighs.

II LIKE A TRAVELER AFTER
A GRIEVOUS CLIMB

Xiao Ge Sails Away

The future has an anchor; the present, a bow.
The past has a boat.
I have a flight to America and a suitcase.

I have space
between my fingers, the lack of knowledge
through which oceans sift.

When I see the airplane, the image is confused
by shimmering heat; and the blood
rising to my face, with the wind.

Gravity is formidable
as a closet of ghosts.

I see from the churning words in my belly
that I will be ill, that I will roll out the window
and hang by the little wheels that have
only a matter of time
before folding.

I have left China. The character for night
looks like bones laughing
among themselves

because I am flying.
In my fingertips are my eyes,
in my skin, a chill, and in the palms
of my hands, the water of my birth.

What Is It?

The view through the window in the air
narrows China into a soft frayed blanket,
a terraced plate of rice,
then a napkin waved briefly as a cloud.

The adventure begins with a plastic tray—
the foreign tongue
explores a small and exactly white cake,
a wedge of butter
stamped with an imperial coat of arms
and a passive continent of beef. I consider

what there is to drink, if "root beer"
will make me drunk enough to transcend
the bland flavors hermetically sealed
in barbaric cellophane.
What is this

moist aromatic square
with edges folded over on itself? As I bite in
it tears away in strands
and clings to the roof of my mouth. I look around
and spit it into my hand, the mess,
the subterfuge, a paper napkin seasoned with perfume.

An Offering

I am a pulse that crouches
as if chickens were let out
above the heart, with shark fins pooled
in a delicate soup from one's own flesh.

Nevertheless I have arrived.

I revolve the new world on a spoon
and think of it as strong medicine, soup
with the smell of fear and nourishment,
and twisted roots.

View From the Chinese Restaurant

1
Culled from the pack: a cigarette.

At dawn,
the cook leans out the window frame:
head scratching, belly scratching.

Two eyes scan the fringes
for a kook driver, a pastier older drunk,

a pair of legs,
or a face he used to know.

2
An old woman peels shrimp.
She hooks the knobs of her fingers
into wooden tines. To save remnants
of scraps.

She reminds her daughter of their lineage
to dynasties. To spoon it in
after the vein is removed.

3
The daughter tries to adjust
a hairpin. How it slips: the silk thread,

the mirror throwing her back,

the waterfall of fluorescence, the vaguest

memories through which she falls
quietly, like paper money.

4

The only customers tonight
are Americans. They expect and they argue:
eenie, meenie, mynie, mo
for equitable shares. We have prepared
our braised ribs. They say *all bone*. *Marrow* we say
aids the blood, toothache,
even starvation. What do they know.
They question salt.

Salt invigorates a taste that we cry for
when we laugh. We are thin,
forgetting to translate for them.
We chop up braised ribs. Thank you
very much, we say as a group. Composed
veneer, our kitchens clean.
Please come again, very soon.

5

By the blue flame of 2 A.M.
a scrap of anger bends the upstairs welder
in front of the sleep not done yet.

What rosins the arm
will solder the China man's
smelly food to the wall;

sparks, then splinters of silence
all at once. Every night,
the thick night racing
under its breath.

How Capable

How broad the air in America, in June.

Dirt scatters where children dig to China
by a picket fence.
Students stretch out on the green

with their eyes closed. But I am uneasy.

Rainwater dissolves in the grass
and becomes an attribute of silence,
or clarity in front of tiger lilies,

or a luxurious bath for pigeons.
But I shift in my shoes
because there are no meetings to attend.

No boundaries to define the scope of my hands.

Taking a long breath below surface,
I feel how capable the trees are.
I feel the alternatives

like open space, a spade
of constricted soil turned, how I can't
imagine who I am, now that I am allowed

the chance to wonder.

Only Religions Change

Everything else is the hunger
that stays the same. And the threadbare aspect
of each darkened afternoon.
In other words, the monastery
has stayed the same.

No thanks,
I'd rather not join the Chinese Methodist
or Presbyterian Church.
Let the imaginative pageant proceed
on its own: the high-wire act of God,
the stone Buddhas
eating rice, shrill points of hysterical beauty
and the pirouettes of Lenin's mind
reincarnated as the Gang of Four.
Please take no offense.
But I've had enough.

I have seen him firsthand,
in his breathtaking orange robes, the Master
full of wisdom, with a yen
for avocados, his mouth opened wide
like a child's. Just so,
they all have insatiable appetites.
I have seen them leave their bodies to lie
submerged with one another, in text
and quotation, hawking recipes for air.

Like a traveler after a grievous climb,
I prefer to live suspended
in disbelief.
And I prefer to love the question, the solitary
inquisitive ache
stretched out over the expanse, *what is it?*
which has always stayed the same.

Prosperous with Birds

Night closes on day, poised
as a cat. Windows shut
into October as on a precipice,

a fate planted by hand
in the dark. With the slow
inheritance of winter,

each day is raised as light
and stirred in shadows.
I have been prosperous

with fatigue and on poor terms
with money. And if I should at last
fail, at least I have had the luck

to see two corners of the world,
and early in the mornings,
to rise beneath departing birds.

When He Raised His Head

Hard to say whether it was forever or not,
but when he lifted his head from the mold of his studies,

he found that the A's were a sullen aptitude
but not required.
When he emerged
from the factory's screaming manufacture of parts
and a busboy's tray of caustic remarks, he wondered
what he was climbing toward.

Part of the earnings accrued
were no more than a habit of suffering.
And when he lifted his head from the books
enough freedom entered his bloodstream to extend
and animate the text.

He could take up dance or figure skating,
and study less. From this vantage, in an empty school yard
under city lights at midnight, he practiced leaps
and spins. On the ice
he began with new, copious notes:

jump with the head raised, lift it up, swing
your arms around to bring the body with you
(don't look down) before landing.

By the Jade Steps

My shoulders wrap around her spine.
She asks, "How did you survive Manchuria?"
The Cultural Revolution
turns into the space between us.

We dance a Viennese waltz,
unfitting to the small room; my arms
materialize too wide.

"Many committed suicide."

Spread in the expansive pose
of a figure skater, practice balance.

Emerald laughter is being mined
from the bottom
of my life.

"This is how it happened:
I kept a verse from an American—
about a road, and there were two ways—
one smaller, and I survived."

I forget my wallet,
umbrella, the feel of a woman's stockings.

"In Detroit," she says, "I would sit
in my closet and read the moon
from a Confucian text."

I talk too loud, like a man
who is deaf.

I lapse in manners.

Jeweled blind
is let down—
the difficult dance patterns, a joy to master.

The Waltz Itself

Loss pivots on the parquet floor.
Just as winter grass
heals a green wound, the waltz leads
to a light circumference

of the room, to what follows
of their knees
as they collide, and their feet
as they confuse themselves

at a threshold for solo
clarinet. Two short steps
propose themselves
into a gloss. And the long

glides into a sleight-of-hand
recovering two minds,
blood soothed
into violins.

Night Vision

1

For a lucent house in a hunched city,
for a solitary man,

several streets lay at hand.
Here a voice without focus
calls, blossoms dust,

and hushes a city. "Where is she?" quiets
the air.

2

Are you asleep already, I wonder.

Back and forth, looking at the sky, the usual stars thrown
at your window, are you asleep now?

I look up with a stiff neck from the middle of the road.
Are you still asleep, is what I think about, leaving
my footprints on the stones.

Seed

We don't talk about private matters; instead
we ask questions that shed light.

Fingers taper across the knees.
Dry lips divide between
whether to say nothing, or whether
what we say has no meaning.

A valley between one word and the next—so long
that mountains separate—our hands
on opposite pages of the album.

One hand points to a slope, and the other
to a view with a woman standing in front:

"Who is she, the one
near you, laughing?" she asks. The stream
flowing between, wild rice in the stream.

Will You Stay?

"After Manchuria, the issue
of whether to come or go
makes little difference," I say.
"I have survived worse."

We stand on the ice. The decision
is to lead with knees bent.
I show her how.

"Careful," I say. An effort
to recall she is married,
with two children.
I have behaved better.

Going backwards and forwards,
a ruse and a mask
for something else.

We are the only ones
on the lake, not what we intended.
"Show me how to stop."

Our voices over the mist,
which is chest high:
"Another time. See you
on the ice." And then the echo,

"See you,"—turn now—
"another time."
The blades, like scissors

on the empty face of a lake.
The clearing in the wake
of where we met, and passed.

To Go

I have thrown my cap in the air among all the others,
as in a flock of blackbirds. As in a parade of celestial bodies.

And finally my heart is permitted travel, to go up in a balloon and lift
from a field like pears in a basket, you and I, an offering at dawn. . . .

To go up without stairs and descend without stairs, with a roar
   of flames
in a puffed-out mouth of colored cloth. . . .

It wouldn't be much alone. How much more it would be with two;
the wind would lean us over the harbor. . . .

But with two more, your children, the drag and tangle of divorce
and nothing to pay the fare? Now we watch what returns to earth

as the next round of dreams. Now we imagine what drifts away
as we wake, with arms laid out as anchors at our sides.

III WHAT STAYS,
WHAT GOES

Momentum

How we arrived at this has nothing to do
with any assertion of right or wrong
scaled to a point of view.

Where we will be has strained
through repair so many times, it's useless
to pretend we know the way.

Footsteps erode underneath us
with all the lights extinguished
going up the stairs.

While asleep, our ears ring
where musicians gathering notes
will not tell its key.

But in the end, where we'll gain momentum,
there is a wellspring,
a velocity of everyday events
and the usual view.

And made there by hand, this moment
alive next to the skin
to transport us.

Verging

1

My hand holds a clearing from the sleeve. Early in spring,
it is the light covering of snow only half covering rain.

I wash my feet in swollen water.
I look for you by the hole in the gate,

sluice way opening, with jeweled fins.

2

Night breathing slow, I lie with you.

I watch my skin for signs of the moon
at odds between building and tree branch,

unsure of limbs,
rising without them through still leaves.

Softness

Rising from sea bottom,
with the back of your hand open,
push against me. My waist will divert you.

A turtle lifts its head; your wrist flexes,

counters the motion of my hand against the back
of your hand. We should breathe
through this gesture, grasp the bird's tail,

a child swinging on a gate, as my voice

finds a common American expression, "Oh my god."
The squeaky gate. The softness inside.
The horse's mane and slanted flying.

Spring Cosmology

Feathered risk. We drift to the city park.
"This is just like Beijing," I say;

"My father, when a political anniversary moved him, would recite
poems in the classical style, '. . . like the sun and moon.'"

A floating risk. And its caution.

"When I began to write poems,
my father criticized them for me: this one is good, this one is bad."

In a haze so light and long to rest, we take
what is feathered out in hand, a sleepless night with a moon.

We pack our things together: the risk, a breeze.

To Lend Another Life to the Ringing of This One

The rose hips here in the bay grow hard; the Canada geese,
the moonstones, and muted stands of pine harden with age.
We both suffered the terms of inheritance.

Years call across the inlet
from the coarse throat of a red-winged blackbird
and we follow, walking close to the waves.

I was drawn to your handmade life as a potter
and a poet. The way you stepped into mud-splattered overalls,
centered the clay, and caused it to rise like silk.

We take stones from a stony beach and throw them out
as far as possible, a miracle of weight
that skips on the water more than twice. I was drawn

to your manner of listening with your head to the side,
making room to know me, believing the bizarre terrain
and the serrated veins of heat ripening underneath.

For Water Birds That Set Out without a Sea

You and I and our unborn child have walked
to look at the shadows of trees, upended rakes
set out above the dam and church yard.

A cormorant lies
with its stretch of neck on the road,
though a goose crosses
with a growth the size of her head
behind her head. She shakes it
again and again, and calls in the night chill
from the stones.

Chewing on a blade of grass, I am distracted
by omens. I taste resin that turns my mouth to chalk,
humming for the bird in my dry hand.

Miscarriage: A Distant Massacre

There is a silence intimate to events—
raw and then distilled—a seepage
internally small that spills only a drop at a time
before it is alarmed
to what might be lost.

There is a not-knowing that recoils from
and returns to events,
and reviews the latent heartbeats,
the growing number of defensive means.

Publicly, the rebellion plays under raised
then lowered eyebrows,
the insupportable probe. "There has been a massacre."
"No! There has been a small but contained
insurrection which is now under control."
The cause defined, as if that
were enough to staunch the flow.

Privately, there is a warning
that we will survive at a distance.
There is a not-talking about nerves and hormones
that quietly disperse the parts of life,
some of which may be renewed,
some of which die trying.

Concerning Children

Her singing changes direction from the rush of air skating past
as she lays them to bed. She is my intimate, foreign heart.

I think of those on the mainland, and my lost child.
The vocal cords, a delicate instrument,

whisper move and turn; so that when I imagine death,
I feel my heel against the edge of the blade

shift weight, glide extended, knees bent to the arms
of our children where they have awakened.

A Letter to Beijing

Now I live in the midwest
and I track telegraph poles to the vanishing point.

My route to work keels to the right or left
because of what I have heard, or haven't heard.

Here everything can only rise in an open field,

and a glut of insoluble heat mounds into the walls
of a glass maze. You should see

how I disappear between streets and corn rows.

Hands behind the wheel,
the mirage in a big car floats across a prairie,
sun-stroked, heart siphoned off by turnings.

At the stoplight, my daughter who is so good at stories
tells me of a sharp-eyed man

from the brown desert who comes
to the blue ocean to drink, without breaking
any rules of transparency. You should see her tell it.

Something About Not Being Safe

Cool my forehead.
Pause for me. I am coming
in a stifled pace and a dearth of sky.

Heat is thick
around the trees, the children's fingers
splayed in the grass, softly,
to the five points of stars.

I am following
the course of a day with diagrams
and blind touch. Stay at hand.

All things move me
to a degree of increase
or dying halfway, and with so much
left to be said. I have grown

too fond. The moon
sighs from the bottom of a well.
Show me home. Soothe me to the door.

What Stays, What Goes

1
With what resolve China
reminds me of children's faces,
as when a cat spreads its fur
while its soft feet pinion
the blue feathers of a bird.

2
Night trains exhale and shriek
against iron rails; a motorcycle
at one A.M. roars off in a trajectory
and returns at two
and leaves at seven and returns at five.

3
A man opens his window
to the sense of lilacs. Spring needs
to be watched and isolated among sounds:
yellow by itself,
purple by itself, warmth alone.

4
Wind feels for the contours,
and envelops the birds' and street's hum
into a blindfold,
and breathes along
the side of my face.

5
A woman lends eloquence
to her feet, leaves the car
and walks along gravel where it interlaces
with grass. Keeping still,
graceful and moist, the landscape arrives.

I Thank You

Do you know
that as light thins in late afternoon
it is you I thank, the you that
sits here as well, listening closely
to a Viennese waltz.

I feel the soles
of my feet, and violins that rise
with a body of instruments
all on loan;

much as a coin tossed
has yet to feel weight, as suddenly as leaves
are just leaves, I am
in the deft wind, in the midst of gravity.

And because it is bad luck
to name what we love, I thank you
for nothing in particular; gold mines dug
out of sleepless nights,
for being fool enough from the start
to safeguard rare days, I dare not say which.

IV INTERNAL STRATEGIES

Once You Are Out in the World

Although the Beijing city bus
shakes us up all the way down Chang An Avenue,
the passengers are transfixed as one
on my wife's Jewish nose
and the magic trick of a half-Chinese baby,
the curly hair—an enigma. Apples, oranges,
can you really add them together?

Someone takes courage to ask the obvious:
who is she to me? Someone else asks, "Can you really
talk to her in the foreign devil's language?"
Another leans over, scolds our child
and pulls the thumb out of her mouth.
"In America, this is considered impolite."

"Is she Russian?" A woman wants to know,
open to the alternative of Mars.
"Once you are out in the world, no one can tell
where you come from. Even a Chinese."

We pass the enormous likeness of Mao in the square,
the mole on his chin the size of an average man.
Bicycles interbreed with taxis, pedestrians. It was foolish
to think I could see the bullet holes
sunk into lampposts as we barreled past.

The glare of sun barely infiltrates the dust,
and one can't help but blink and nod over the view.
Out of the corner of my eye, I catch sight of a banner
over a storefront: Accumulate Celestial Dollars Restaurant.

Times have changed. Our child has been lulled
to sleep, the world leveled by its revolutions. She clings
to her perfect thumb, half in, half out;
and at the next jolt of changing gears,
gravity itself will let it fall.

The Last Piece

1. The Butcher

If you're not related and you've come
for a good cut of meat, it's useless to ask
for lean or fat; in a discreet way

know to use finesse, gauge

as he cuts, that he will get to the good part
when he gets to you.

Walk the airless market, waiting
with an eye trained on the cleaver as he cuts

from either end and spreads the slabs,
takes in orders, divides among us. Line up

at the right time and hope,

when you get there,
for the leanest piece.

2. The Surgeon

As they arrived through the night

we divided and spread them
lined up, taking limbs through
their separate sleeves, deflated socks,

and blind endeavors.
Before we could remove the bullets

relatives came, knowing

to use finesse, gauging correctly
that all names registered that night
would be used against them.

It was the wrong time to be wounded.
Even the dead were taken home.
We are short-changed

from either end: trained only to heal.
And so we wait for our chance.

The discrete hope lying there,
cut down to the leanest piece.

The Street of Embroiderers

Our great leader on stilts can repair
the eyes of needles. The heat of ideology
causes his skin to pull taut with longing
over the governing design.

The words surrounding us rise
into floral relief over our drab,
gray street. A swath of phrases
separates fair from unfair in painstaking silk

and when he shouts, we, the embroiderers
stitch like devils. How quickly
arguments are covered over. Old concerns
thicken with a grudge while our heads

bend over a length of thread.
And then he gradually begins to age, to weave.
None so close as to catch
the little man. And judging the distance

his falling will take forever. We have grieved
but people come for souvenirs,
a new economy, and we're growing rich
with work lined up for years.

Two Performances at Beihai Park

1. A Shopkeeper from Nanjing Demonstrates the Art of Mind Control

We were close enough
to hear his muscles as he walked on stage with several spears,
thin as needles, in a sack. We shifted in our shoes;

his feet at a harmonious distance, eyes turned
into center.

For some time, we watched from the inside of his body
as it grew more heated.
We mumbled, and centrifugal force from a murmur
traveled along his thighs.

We felt great pain and a shout, as he thrust a spear through his arm
and another through his leg;

four and five, but no blood.
He pulled us out, which made us tremble like water and turn away.

And then he bowed, aware now
of his audience, and clattered the spears in his hand.

2. The Contortionist

We could have
gone to yet another event
and missed the wrongdoing of her spine,
and her extremities holding candle flame
in a throw and catch of grace.
Her small feet, sensitive
to the heat that stroked them, peeled back

and exchanged themselves for hands.
Our nerves drenched in our palms.
She arranged her bones as feathers
and added a smile, too red,
too warm for its measure
should it fall.

In the second half
of her act (how long
this took!), she leaned toward us
and wheeled a backward arch
out of the mouth-petals
of a huge metallic rose.
And we opened our mouths.
Some wondered about the acrobats they might
have seen. What did they do?
In a glazed trance, our eyes shed
pods of diminished light.
Could we have missed something?
The crowds dispersed.
We should have waited
until the end, and asked her
how she did it, how she subverted
the face of nature like that,
and at what cost.

Graffiti at the Peak of Folded Brocade Hill

Overlooking Li River after tourists
have left because of rain,
a man watches the half-light
spawn peace out of an aberration of time.

Who will listen
to a violinist who for thirteen
years was assigned the job
of butchering pigs?

Far below, the city's gravel
bleeds into the green ribbon of river
that yawns through a thousand
years of indifference.

Clouds and mountains meet.
He follows the old Masters' brush spirited
into rock that laments the corruption
of Tang officials.

Carving underneath,
dust flying off in a thousand directions,
the river runs away, his hands,
their music, beyond reach.

No Personal Power

Leading into the bus, a young woman
takes her designer umbrella as gauntlet
and pries a curve of air
between multiple arms
and shoulders. Over her head
and advancing, a young man bristles
with sunglasses, fake
Rolex and rings. A briefcase
with severe weight at four corners
edges her out of the way.
The sheer corruption
of shopping bags shoves aside raw
nerves carried backwards
and further back, my own mind
crowded out and lost. Where
is my wife's hand? The heat, a slippery
hold; a man shouts,
Make way for our foreign guest!
Another, *Why the hell should I?*
Who cares? Unable to direct
or fall, my pulse implies
that I have just entered prison
by some terrible
mistake, the bars pressing
against the valves of my heart, the doors
sliding shut. Nothing's changed,
I explain to her later.
I should have known.

Internal Strategy

By 7 A.M., Qi Gung class for cancer patients is over.
Most of us are old and we leave the square slowly,
with hands swaying out from our sides

to cultivate our magnetic "Qi," clarity
among endless pedestrians. The young disco
and social dancers near us,

they lose their strength quickly. Their radios glare
with the western dance craze. Whereas our patience
resolves upon the swanlike motion in the palms,

containing air, pushing it out, and lifting shoulders
with subtle, incipient force.
We keep the arms slightly away

from the body. Focused on vital energy.
Fingers separate from each other. Assuming
the silence of witness, we are breathing past

the dancers as they assemble, pair off
and tango at arm's length. Our neck
and back, internal organs are relaxed.

Qi Gung, our master says, cures disease
and even the ancestry of disease. With Qi Gung
it is possible to forgo food, become invisible in a massacre

and survive, like the best dancer's yellow shoes
in a fox trot, raising dust. Like her thin yellow dress,
so alive around her young bones.

An Old Recipe

With what	my last	and my
I have	grandchild	daughter-in-law
I hold	so that you	can go out

1. I pour my voice over her skin and stroke her entire back in the spoon of my palm;   2. the baby's keen sense of loss,   3. the clarity in her tears stirs an old man with false teeth and fragile heart to put on slippers with haste and walk her in the courtyard   4. endlessly   5. until you return. And that she deigns to rest on my shoulder melts caution out of an old Cadre's bones so that I will   6. show her anything: the alley's weeds, suspicious neighbors, stray pigs and dogs, Party directives pasted to the walls, or raucous cicadas in the trees if it is what   7. she desires.

Most Famous Beauty Spot in All of China

We catch the local bus
squeezed among newlyweds
making pilgrimage
to West Lake, legendary pool
shimmering at dawn,
        to three pagodas
mirroring the moon
and the place where oars are stilled
by hanging moss
and the delicate cloth of water lilies.
At the docks,
        private entrepreneurs
sing, *Low price, low price, see all
for 20 yuan!* Released
to an island, we are hemmed in on all sides
by a sea of others arriving.
        Overloaded ferries
kneel to the wharf with foreboding,
but no one is concerned. A woman laughs
as a young man runs over her shoe.
Someone lights incense
in the sand.
        A queue for the crooked bridge,
for a photo by a plaque.
From a clearing in the trees,
a dance class has begun, and a waltz
set to the music of "Here
Comes the Bride."
        And so we spin
within range of the tape cassette,
in between souvenirs, on the fringes
of the vendors' calls shimmering
through the heat.

Perhaps Li Bai
composed a poem on this very spot.
What an idea. In three-quarter time,
I will sing one in your ear.

To Dance Like This

Eyes pine for field, hands
swing from the waist
as if the sun were close to evening
on a warm night.

They swing as graceful and slow
as turtles walking across mud flats,
with a wet sheen
reflected on their shells.

Leave your right foot in the place
where your left used to be, as lightly
as this, again in reverse. Sea gulls
are inspired, with the moon in place.

Clams in the narrows
raise their necks to surface
as one breath through a thousand
vital holes. Their heads remain in thrall

to the ethereal body. Bend
into the right with the right knee,
turn into the line of direction.
And the line disappears

by the gratitude of arms
that curve the air higher. Extend,
and the appropriate bones water with love
and the final count clicks heels.

To Keep Us Listening Forever

The land turns up a corrugated iron face lathered in fog.

We come between revolution and the cold.
Now comes our time.
Green takes on an alias, and listening,
we imagine using ideas
in order to live beyond our means.
Our shelter

falls out of the trees
as leaves backslide, mumbling into pools.
Wind draws out a landscape to a thread.
But rather than miss dreaming

we will lean against the horizon and shove. There is only
a blue shred of it left, a deep breath
wherein we name children and invoke heroes.

Down the last visible hole of light,
the sun pans for gold, settling for amethyst, then coal.
Never mind. An alibi for dawn
will keep us listening for those who know
how to defer the cost, at any cost.

Reading What I See

I fold a corner of the page.
Tomorrow we fly home to America . . . today
I read to an old Party informant near death.

My father's neighbor for thirty years, and only now
he admits to this weakness for classical
Chinese poems. He leans his ear
toward me without restraint, arms creased
into the pillows by his head.

From the thin membranes
of his voice, as from twin birds, he intones
a classical response, *thank you*, over
and over.

A thread between near strangers or enemies,
as in what I have done or said for longing
in the past—this is the needle,
the sudden detail that rises from my mouth
without thinking it over first: *it's okay,
I thank you too.*

Like poetry after reading, I stand
in the neighbor's bedroom at a loss;
a carpet, a concrete floor
laid out over the earth.

The tormented man climbs the pillars
of a four-poster bed. Gratefully
he rises between them, out of a cauldron
of black ink, his skin
like wet and then dried rice paper.

EPILOGUE

The Love Poems of an Emperor's Concubine

1
She writes a line of verse, "I am old . . . ," and lifts the brush;
overwhelming twilight dissolves in water,
her presence diffused by a swift railing arched
over a pool in black ink.

The smallest sound of her brush
is only the night singing along a worn path. In one direction,
to her lord, in another to her children's mouths open in sleep.
Ink dries on the edge of her stone.

2
She sees the night pierced through by morning.
She breathes in the pavilion and considers the landscape
with a whip of her sleeve as her hand pushes free.

Slow is elegant.
In the softness inside a gesture, she sips tea.

As one of the oldest, she knows to extend herself
beyond changes in domestic climate, to the watchfulness
of her breath, to the particular grace of a metaphor.

3
Spirit money for the dead flies into trade.
With longing, children are let out in the courtyard
on strings of coins
and the draft of a lover's dialogue.

Every word comes to what can't be spared.
She scarcely moves while searching
for the rhyme that is discrete and ripples out.

She watches a magpie as it hops
along the bamboo slats of a rail, marking
her portion of the emperor's wealth, her version
of the deed to be written out entirely in verse.

NOTES

Notes

Ghost Marriage: In Taiwan and some remote parts of mainland China an ancient ritual is still being performed wherein two families will marry off their deceased children. A wedding complete with food, guests, and celebration is carried out at the cemetery. This is seen as a way to correct the misfortune of having offspring die before having a chance to marry and carry on the family line.

The Son of Heaven: The epigraph is taken from a poem that Mao composed and addressed to a fellow poet in 1949 during the celebrations marking the Communist victory in China. Emperors were usually referred to as "The Son of Heaven," and Mao has been similarly compared.

About Brilliance: In 1956, as an effort to promote Party rectification and include the intellectuals in the government's struggle for unity, Mao proclaimed "big democracy" with his famous slogan, "Let a Hundred Flowers Bloom, Let a Hundred Schools of Thought Contend." As criticism of the Party mounted, Mao quickly turned this open policy into a tremendous purge to punish those who spoke against him. Soon after came The Great Leap Forward, a campaign that resulted in starvation (approximately twenty million people died in one year alone) and nearly destroyed the country's economy.

Xiao Ge Wants to Be a Hero: Before the onset of the Cultural Revolution was a time of high moral standards. Children idolized heroes of the war years, such as Dong Chun Rei. Dong was born a poor peasant abused by landlords. He joined the Communist guerrilla movement against Chiang Kai-shek and later joined the PLA (People's Liberation Army). In a fierce battle with the PLA advancing across an open terrain and Chiang Kai-shek's troops protected on a bridge, the PLA was losing nearly everyone until Dong Chun Rei made the ultimate sacrifice. He raced under the bridge and, using his body, raised a pack of dynamite above his head to the height needed to blow up the bridge. Just before setting it off, he shouted, "For the new China! Forward!"

The Theme: The italicized phrase beginning, "you have heard of using wings to fly . . ." is taken from Chuang-tzu's Inner Chapters.

The Day Tiananmen Square Filled with Shoes: At the onset of the Cultural Revolution in 1966, mass rallies for the Red Guards were held in Tiananmen Square. When Chairman Mao addressed the crowds that packed the square (ninety-eight acres), the young people's enthusiasm was so great that many were trampled in their effort to reach Mao. After the rallies, truckloads of shoes had to be carted away.

The Lost Generation: During the Cultural Revolution, approximately fourteen million young people were sent to the countryside, ostensibly to help the peasants and be "re-educated" by them. The "cow shed" was the term used for the hard-labor camps where cadres were sent to be "re-educated." Many families were split apart and sent to different parts of the country, without any chance for contact, often for years.

What We Know about Waves: Because of the famine resulting from the Great Leap Forward in 1958, there were several campaigns and sometimes bizarre remedies set out to patch the disaster. In one instance, Mao decided that too many birds were eating the seed that the farmers planted, so he ordered the entire country to bang pots and pans for three days and nights. This forced the birds to fly up in the sky until they eventually died of exhaustion.

Cat Show in Factory #2: After one year in Manchuria, Xiao Ge was granted leave to go home for a visit. Rather than return to the harsh conditions of Manchuria, Xiao Ge stayed home on the pretext of illness. Later he had to hide in his own home because he no longer had a resident permit for Beijing. As a last-ditch effort at controlling his fate, he took up the violin. Many young people practiced hard at musical instruments at this time, not necessarily for the love of music but because the best musicians were recruited into the Red Army and thereby granted an easier life, and resident permits for wherever they liked. In Xiao Ge's case, at the age of sixteen he was already too old to become an accomplished musician. Finally, thanks to some backdoor influence from his father, he was able to find "safe" factory work in southern China.

Growing Up on the Sly: Xiao Ge, as one of the Lost Generation, had no formal education beyond sixth grade. Schooling was, for all practical purposes, abandoned for the ten-year period of the Cultural Revolution. In the 1970s, while working a factory job in Xing Tai as a machinist's apprentice, Xiao Ge taught himself algebra, trigonometry, and calculus.

Miscarriage: A Distant Massacre: A few days after the Tiananmen Square massacre, Deng Xiaoping gave a speech that justified the actions of the army and transferred the blame away from the common people. His explanations, "fate" and "the influence of bad elements," seemed to contradict and cancel each other out, as this translated excerpt shows: "It was bound to happen and was independent of man's will. . . . Actually, what we faced was not just some ordinary people who were misguided, but also a rebellious clique and a large quantity of the dregs of society."

The Last Piece: Many of those who were taken to hospitals after the Tiananmen Square massacre were secretly taken away by relatives. This was to avoid having the wounded registered, which would implicate them later. Even the dead, once registered, could cause trouble for the surviving families.

Most Famous Beauty Spot in All of China: The poem refers to West Lake, in Hangzhou, which has been one of the most famous tourist spots in China for many centuries. Many famous poets have been known to travel to West Lake. Li Bai, 701–762, known in the west as Li Po, was considered to be one of the most gifted poets in China. A free-spirited, wandering man who never held any official post, he loved to drink wine and was beloved and supported by his many friends and relatives because of his unique talent for joy and poetry. It is said that he died by falling from a boat while trying to embrace the reflection of the moon.

About the Author

A native of Detroit, Anita Feng now lives in Champaign, Illinois, where she is a ceramic artist. She earned her B.A. in English and her M.F.A. in Creative Writing from Brown University. Among her awards are the Pablo Neruda Prize and an NEA Fellowship.

About the Book

Internal Strategies was designed and typeset on a Macintosh in Quark XPress by Kachergis Book Design of Pittsboro, North Carolina. The typeface, Zapf Humanist, is a digitized rendition of Optima. Herman Zapf designed Optima in 1956, and in 1986 he oversaw the digitization of Zapf Humanist at Bitstream.

Internal Strategies was printed on sixty-pound Glatfelter Supple Opaque Recycled and bound by Thomson-Shore, Inc., Dexter, Michigan.